CURRICULUM AND EVALUATION

S T A N D A R D S

FOR SCHOOL MATHEMATICS
ADDENDA SERIES, GRADES K–6

F I R S T - G R A D E B O O K

Grace Burton

Douglas Clements

Terrence Coburn

John Del Grande

John Firkins

Jeane Joyner

Miriam A. Leiva

Mary M. Lindquist

Lorna Morrow

Miriam A. Leiva, Series Editor

NATIONAL COUNCIL OF
TEACHERS OF MATHEMATICS

Library of Congress Cataloging-in-Publication Data:

First-grade book / Grace Burton ... [et al.].
    p.   cm. — (Curriculum and evaluation standards for school
mathematics addenda series. Grades K–6)
    Includes bibliographical references.
    ISBN 0-87353-309-7 (set). — ISBN 0-87353-311-9 (v. 1)
    1. Mathematics—Study and teaching (Elementary)   I. Burton, Grace
M.   II. National Council of Teachers of Mathematics.   III. Series.
QA135.5.F5 1991
372.7—dc20   91-25729
                                    CIP

Photographs are by Patricia Fisher; artwork is by Lynn Gohman and Don Christian.

Printed in the United States of America

FOREWORD

The *Curriculum and Evaluation Standards for School Mathematics* (NCTM 1989a) describes a framework for revising and strengthening school mathematics. This visionary document provides a set of guidelines for K–12 mathematics curricula and for evaluating both the mathematics curriculum and students' progress. It not only addresses what mathematics students should learn but also how they should learn it.

As the document was being developed, it became apparent that supporting publications would be needed to interpret and illustrate how the vision could be translated realistically into classroom practices. A Task Force on the Addenda to the Curriculum and Evaluation Standards for School Mathematics, chaired by Thomas Rowan and composed of Joan Duea, Christian Hirsch, Marie Jernigan, and Richard Lodholz, was appointed by Shirley Frye, then NCTM president. The Task Force's recommendations on the scope and nature of the supporting publications were submitted to the Educational Materials Committee, which subsequently framed the Addenda Project.

Central to the Addenda Project was the formation of three writing teams—consisting of classroom teachers, mathematics supervisors, and university mathematics educators—to prepare a series of publications, the Addenda Series, targeted at mathematics instruction in grades K–6, 5–8, and 9–12. The purpose of the series is to clarify and illustrate the message of the *Curriculum and Evaluation Standards*. The underlying themes of problem solving, reasoning, communication, and connections are woven throughout the materials, as is the view of assessment as a means of guiding instruction. Activities have been field tested by teachers to ensure that they reflect the realities of today's classrooms.

It is envisioned that the Addenda Series will be a source of ideas by teachers as they begin to implement the recommendations in the NCTM *Curriculum and Evaluation Standards*. Individual volumes in the series are appropriate for in-service programs and for preservice courses in teacher education programs.

A project of this magnitude required the efforts and talents of many people over an extended time. Sincerest appreciation is extended to the authors and the editor and to the following teachers who played key roles in developing, revising, and trying out the materials for the *First-Grade Book*: Angela C. Gardner, Liana C. Holton, and Ann Mills.   Finally, this project would not have materialized without the outstanding technical support supplied by Cynthia Rosso and the NCTM publications staff.

Bonnie H. Litwiller
Addenda Project Coordinator

PREFACE

Something exciting is happening in many elementary school classrooms! A vision of an innovative mathematics program is coming alive. There *is* a shift in emphasis in the teaching and learning of mathematics. Teachers are encouraging children to investigate, discuss, question, and verify. They are focusing on explorations and dialogues. They are using various strategies to assess students' progress. They are making mathematics accessible to all children while exposing them to the value and the beauty of mathematics. Teachers and students are excited, and their enthusiasm is contagious. You can *catch it* when you hear children confidently explaining their solutions to the class, when you see them modeling problems with manipulatives, and when you observe them using a variety of methods and materials to arrive at answers. Some children are working with paper and pencil or with calculators; others are sharpening their estimation and mental math skills. There is noise in these classrooms—the sounds of students actively participating in the class and constructing their own knowledge through experiences that will give them confidence in their own abilities and make them mathematically powerful.

> I remember my own experiences in mathematics in elementary school. The classroom was quiet; all you could hear was the movement of pencils across sheets of paper and an occasional comment from the teacher. I was often bored; work was done in silent isolation, rules were memorized, and many routine problems were worked using rules few of us understood. Mathematics didn't always make sense. It was something that you did in school, mostly with numbers, and that you didn't need outside the classroom.
>
> "Why are we doing this?" my friend whispered.
>
> "Because it's in the book," I replied.
>
> "Do it this way," the teacher would explain while writing another problem on the chalkboard. "When you finish, work the next ten problems in the book."

We must go beyond how we were taught and teach how we wish we had been taught. We must bring to life a vision of what a mathematics classroom should be.

Rationale for Change

These are challenging times for you, the teachers of elementary school mathematics, and for your students. Major reforms in school mathematics are advocated in reports that call for changes in the curriculum, in student and program evaluations, in instruction, and in the classroom environment. These reforms are prompted by the changing needs of our society, which demand that all students become mathematically literate to function effectively in a technological world. A richer mathematics program is also supported by an explosion of new mathematical knowledge—more mathematics has been created in this century than in all our previous history. Research studies on teaching and learning, with emphasis on *how children learn mathematics,* have had a significant impact on current practices and strengthen the case for reform. Advances in technology also dictate changes in content and teaching.

Our students, the citizens of tomorrow, need to learn not only *more* mathematics but also mathematics that is broader in scope. They must have a strong academic foundation to enable them to expand their knowledge, to interpret information, to make reasonable decisions, and to solve increasingly complex problems using various approaches and tools, including calculators and computers. Mathematics instruction must reflect and implement these revised educational goals and increased expectations.

The blueprint for reform is the *Curriculum and Evaluation Standards for School Mathematics* (NCTM 1989a), which identifies a set of standards for the mathematics curriculum in grades K–12 as well as standards for evaluating the quality of programs and students' performance. The *Curriculum and Evaluation Standards* sets forth a bold vision of what mathematics education in grades K–12 should be and describes how mathematics classrooms can fit the vision.

"My clown has circles, triangles, and rectangles."

Mathematics as Sense Making

In the past, mathematics classrooms were dominated by instruction and performance of rote procedures "to get the right answer." The *Curriculum and Evaluation Standards* supports the view of school mathematics as a sense-making experience encompassing a wide range of content, instructional approaches, and evaluation techniques.

Four standards are closely woven into content and instruction: mathematics as problem solving, mathematics as communication, mathematics as reasoning, and mathematical connections. These strands are common themes that support all other standards throughout all grade levels.

A primary goal for the study of mathematics is to give children experiences that promote the ability *to solve problems* and that build mathematics from situations generated within the context of everyday experiences. Students are also expected *to make conjectures and conclusions* and *to discuss their reasoning* in words, both written and spoken; with pictures, graphs, and charts; and with manipulatives. Moreover, students learn *to value mathematics* when they *make connections* between topics in mathematics, between the concrete and the abstract, between concepts and skills, and between mathematics and other areas in the curriculum.

Yolanda, a student in the bilingual program remembers: "I didn't understand everything Mr. Sanchez was saying, but when he made a pattern with pictures and blocks, I made one just like his! I understood!"

The Changing Roles of Students

Previous efforts to reform school mathematics focused primarily on the curriculum; the *Curriculum and Evaluation Standards* also deals with other factors—in particular, students—that affect and are affected by reforms. The role of students is redirected from passive recipients to active participants, from isolated workers to team members, from listeners to investigators and reporters, and from timid followers to intrepid explorers and risk takers. They are asked to develop, discuss, create, model, validate, and investigate to learn mathematics.

Many people, including students, believe that mathematics is for the privileged few. It is time to dispel that myth. All children, regardless of sex, socioeconomic background, language, race, or ethnic origin, can and must succeed in school mathematics. With proper instruction, encouragement, and high expectations, *all* students can do mathematics.

Your Role in Implementing the Standards

All elementary school teachers are teachers of mathematics. Thus, your role is to build your students' self-confidence and nurture their natural curiosity; to challenge them with rich problems through which they will learn to value mathematics and appreciate the order and beauty of mathematics; to provide them with a strong foundation for further study; and to encourage their mathematical ability and power.

The elementary school years are crucial in a child's cognitive and affective development, and you are the central figure. You structure classroom experiences to implement the curriculum and create a supportive

"We need one more block to make the same building on the other side of the street."

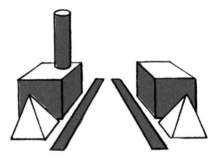

environment for learning to take place. In most activities you are the guide, the coach, the facilitator, and the instigator of mathematical explorations.

♦ You give children the gift of self-confidence. Through your careful grouping, astute questions, appropriate tasks, and realistic expectations, each student can experience success.

♦ Long after they forget childhood events, your students will remember you. Your excitement and interest permeate the room and stimulate their appreciation for mathematics.

♦ Through your classroom practices, you promote mathematical thinking, reasoning, and understanding.

♦ You lay the foundation on which further study will take place. You give students multiple strategies and tools to solve problems. The questions you ask and the problems you pose can capture your students' imagination, arouse their curiosity, and encourage their creativity.

♦ You facilitate the building of their knowledge by giving them interesting problems to solve, which leads to the development of concepts and important mathematical ideas.

♦ Rules, algorithms, and formulas emerge from student explorations guided by you, the teacher of mathematics.

Instructional Tools and the Standards

In order to implement the curriculum envisioned in the *Curriculum and Evaluation Standards,* we must carefully select and creatively use instructional tools. The textbook is only one of many important teaching resources. Children's development of concepts is fostered by their extensive use of physical materials to represent and describe mathematical ideas.

Calculators and computers are essential instructional tools at all levels. Through the appropriate use of these tools, students are able to solve realistic problems, investigate patterns, explore procedures, and focus on the steps to solve problems instead of on tedious computations.

Implementing the Evaluation Standards

Evaluation must be an integral part of teaching. A primary component of instruction is an ongoing assessment of what goes on in our classrooms. This information helps us make decisions about what we teach and how we teach it, about students' progress and feelings, and about our mathematics program.

"My pattern is the same as yours, but I used different pictures."

The *Curriculum and Evaluation Standards* advocates many changes in curriculum, in instruction, and in the roles of students and teachers. None of these changes are more important than those related to evaluation. We must learn to use a variety of assessment instruments and not depend on pencil-and-paper tests alone. Tools such as observations, interviews, projects, reports, portfolios, diaries, and tests provide a more complete picture of what children understand and are able to use. Knowing what questions to ask is a skill we must develop.

When we test, we send a message about what we think is important. Because we encourage reasoning and communicating mathematically, we practice these skills. Because manipulatives and calculators are valuable tools for learning, we promote their use in the classroom. Because we want children to experience cooperative problem solving, we provide opportunities for group activities. *Not only must we evaluate what we want children to learn, but also how we want them to learn it.*

You and This Book

This booklet is part of the Curriculum and Evaluation for School Mathematics Addenda Series, Grades K–6. This series was designed to illustrate the standards and to help you translate them into classroom practice through—

♦ sample lessons and discussions that focus on the development of concepts;

♦ activities that connect models and manipulatives with concepts and with mathematical representations;

♦ problems that exemplify the use and integration of technology;

♦ teaching strategies that promote students' reasoning;

♦ approaches to evaluate students' progress;

♦ techniques to improve instruction.

In this booklet, both traditional and new topics are explored in four areas: Patterns, Number Sense and Operations, Making Sense of Data, and Geometry and Spatial Sense.

You will find that certain classic first-grade activities, such as classifying patterns, exploring number patterns, representing numbers in various ways, estimating, organizing data, measuring, and investigating geometry in the world around us, have been injected with an investigative flavor. You will also encounter a variety of problems and questions to explore with your first-graders. Margin notes give you additional information on the activities and on such topics as student self-confidence, evaluation, and grouping. Connections to science, language arts, social studies, and other areas in the curriculum are made throughout. Supporting statements from the *Curriculum and Evaluation Standards* appear as margin notes.

Change is an ongoing process that takes time and courage. It is not easy to go beyond comfort and security to try new things. As you use this book, pick and choose at will, and sample alternative approaches and ideas for instruction and assessment. Savor the freedom of change. All the documents in the world will not effect change in the classrooms; *only you can.*

The Challenge and the Vision

"I wonder why...?"

"What would happen if ...?" "Tell me about your pattern."

"Can you do it another way?" "Our group has a different solution."

These inviting words give students the freedom to be creative, the confidence to solve problems, and the power to do mathematics. When you give your students the opportunity to construct their own knowledge, you are opening the doors of mathematics to *all* young learners.

This is the challenge. This is the vision.

Miriam A. Leiva, Editor
K–6 Addenda Series

"If I use bigger ladybugs, I don't need as many to cover the leaves."

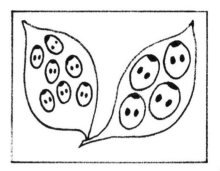

"I wonder in how many different ways we could dress the snowmen if we had scarves and hats of two different colors."

BIBLIOGRAPHY

National Council of Teachers of Mathematics. Curriculum and Evaluation Standards for School Mathematics Addenda Series, Grades K–6, edited by Miriam A. Leiva. Reston, Va.: The Council, 1991.

___. Curriculum and Evaluation Standards for School Mathematics Addenda Series, Grades 5–8, edited by Frances R. Curcio. Reston, Va.: The Council, 1991.

___. Curriculum and Evaluation Standards for School Mathematics Addenda Series, Grades 9–12, edited by Christian R. Hirsch. Reston, Va.: The Council, 1991.

___. Curriculum and Evaluation Standards for School Mathematics. Reston, Va.: The Council, 1989a.

___. New Directions for Elementary School Mathematics. 1989 Yearbook of the National Council of Teachers of Mathematics. Edited by Paul Trafton. Reston, Va.: The Council, 1989b.

___. Professional Standards for Teaching Mathematics. Reston, Va.: The Council, 1991.

National Research Council. Everybody Counts: A Report to the Nation on the Future of Mathematics Education. Washington, D.C.: National Academy Press, 1989.

ACKNOWLEDGMENTS

At a time when the mathematics community was looking for directions on implementing the Curriculum and Evaluation Standards for School Mathematics, a group of dedicated professionals agreed to serve on the NCTM Elementary Addenda Project.

The task of editing and writing for this series has been challenging and rewarding. Selecting, testing, writing, and editing, as we attempted to translate the message of the Standards into classroom practices, proved to be a monumental and ambitious task. It could not have been done without the dedication and hard work of the authors, the teachers who reviewed and field tested the activities, and the editorial team.

My appreciation is extended to the main authors for each topic:

Grace Burton	Number Sense and Operations
Terrence Coburn	Patterns
John Del Grande and Lorna Morrow	Geometry and Spatial Sense
Mary M. Lindquist	Making Sense of Data

Our colleagues in the classrooms, Angela Gardner, Liana Holton, and Ann Mills, are thanked for giving us the unique perspective of teachers and children.

A special note of gratitude is owed to the individuals who served both as writers and as the editorial panel: Douglas Clements, John Firkins, and Jeane Joyner.

The editor also gratefully acknowledges the strong support of Bonnie Litwiller, Coordinator of the Addenda Project, and the assistance of Cynthia Rosso and the NCTM production staff for their guidance and help through the process of planning and producing this series of books.

The greatest reward for all who have contributed to this effort will be the knowledge that the ideas presented here have been implemented in elementary school classrooms, that these ideas have made realities out of visions, and that they have fostered improved mathematics programs for all children.

Miriam A. Leiva

PATTERNS

Patterns weave mathematical topics together. Through the study of patterns, children learn to see relationships and make connections, generalizations, and predictions about the world around them. Working with patterns nurtures the kind of mathematical thinking that empowers children to solve problems confidently and relate new situations to previous experiences.

First-grade patterning activities are often extensions of those used earlier. The focus in kindergarten is on repetition of events or designs using sound, motion, shape, and quantity. In the first grade there is continued emphasis on extending patterns and transferring them from one medium to another.

Seeing many different representations of the same pattern helps children learn to generalize and recognize patterns in broader contexts. Noting similarities and differences in several examples of the same pattern develops skill in using pattern recognition to solve problems.

Some activities challenge students to determine a missing piece of a pattern rather than just to extend the pattern. Students then see the "whole" picture in the same way they understand the meaning of a word in the context in which it is used. When counting is integrated with pattern activities, children's mathematical experiences are further enriched. In addition, children's reasoning skills are developed through answering such questions as "What do you think should come next?"; "Why do you think that is a good answer?"; or "Can you explain this pattern in another way?"

The pattern activities offered here rely primarily on physical objects and pictures. They encourage children to strengthen their communication skills through oral descriptions of their patterns and they supply a natural link between mathematics and other disciplines.

PATTERN STAMPING

Get ready. The purpose of this activity is to have children create and extend patterns. Children identify basic pattern units and use them to create linear patterns. They will need rubber stamps, stamp pads, and paper. Rubber stamps are available through catalogs, toy stores, and teacher supply stores. Stamps representing many subjects, such as animals, toys, and shapes, allow this activity to be integrated into several themes. The students also need a strip of paper only long enough to stamp no more than four times and another strip about three feet long. The short strip will be used to show the pattern unit. Adding-machine tape or other long strips of paper will enable the children to repeat their linear patterns.

From the earliest grades. the curriculum should give students opportunities to focus on regularities in events, shapes, designs, and sets of numbers. Children should begin to see that regularity is the essence of mathematics. (NCTM 1989a, p.60)

Incorporate children's literature with the work on patterns by reading "The Princess and the Pea" and having children design a display to tell the story. Strips with linear patterns become the mattresses on which the girls slept.

Beneath the stacks of mattresses glue a large bean or pea and have children write about the patterns they made for their mattresses.

Stamping a single figure continuously on a long strip of paper is a simple pattern with many applications. For example, children can create nonstandard measuring tapes using single stamps.

Get going. Tell the students to decide on a design (a unit to repeat) and to stamp it on the short strip. Let different children show their designs to the class and tell about them.

These are such pretty designs. Why don't we repeat them on long strips of paper?

Give the students time to reproduce their designs and create linear patterns.

Have the students share how they have repeated their designs to make the long strips. Reinforce the idea that the designs on the short pieces of paper are the basic units used to create the linear pattern.

Keep going. Because children need many experiences with patterns, you will want to establish a place in the classroom that has different materials for them to use in making more designs. They can use patterns to make measuring tapes, headbands or belts, borders on placemats or picture frames, book covers, bulletin board borders, and wrapping paper. Have the children work in pairs, and encourage them to produce several products with their partners, sharing all materials. Provide a time and a place for the students to display their products and talk about what they have done.

After the students demonstrate the ability to identify basic pattern units at concrete and pictorial levels, they can be given independent projects that might include pencil-and-paper tasks such as the worksheet illustrated.

TRANSLATING PATTERNS

Get ready. The purpose of this activity is to have children translate patterns from one medium into another. Children will identify basic pattern units and create new representations of the patterns.

For this activity you will need connecting cubes and, if possible, a recording of the song "Old McDonald Had a Farm." You may also want to make various sample patterns that are large enough for the entire class to see.

The song "There's a Hole in the Bottom of the Sea" is another example of a growing pattern. Beginning with a line that says "There's a log in the hole in the bottom of the sea," the song continues and builds to "There's a hair on the wart on the frog on the limb on the log in the hole in the bottom of the sea."

Get going. Children enjoy singing "Old McDonald Had a Farm" and making the animal sounds in the story. After they sing the song, ask the children to talk about how patterns help them to remember the song.

Using the sounds that the animals make, explore different patterns that could be created. Suggest both repeating and growing patterns. For example, "meow-meow-quack, meow-meow-quack" is a repeating pattern. A growing pattern might be "meow-quack, meow-quack-quack, meow-quack-quack-quack." After the children have repeated the pattern several times, ask for volunteers to create new patterns for their classmates. Record these patterns on language experience charts for the children to repeat on their own or at another time with the group.

When the children feel comfortable with the oral patterns, help them translate the sounds into color patterns with the connecting cubes. For example, ask questions such as these:

What color would you like for the cat's sound? How many cubes will we need each time we come to that sound?

What color cubes shall we use to represent the duck's sound?

Ask the children to tell other ways to represent their animal sound patterns, such as actions with claps and snaps. Show the children sample patterns on the overhead projector or the chalkboard.

△ ☐ △ ☐ △ ☐   ☆ ☆ ○ ☆ ☆ ○   ● ● ○ ○ ○ ● ● ○ ○

Discuss with the children what the basic pattern unit is in each sequence and how they might turn the designs into patterns with animal sounds.

How could you name the designs using letters of the alphabet?

What pattern units are repeated?

If I use the letter A instead of the circle and the letter B instead of the square, how would I write these patterns?

Keep going. Give the children materials such as colored self-adhesive circles, toothpicks and glue, scraps of construction paper, and crayons and markers for copying given patterns in several different media. You might have children work in pairs to encourage discussion of the patterns. Each student needs four paper strips ten to twelve inches long.

Model a pattern for the children by using objects such as teddy bear counters or a large sample pattern you have made. Tell the children to show the same pattern in four different ways on their strips of paper. Before they begin, encourage them to talk with their partner about the pattern unit and how they plan to represent it. When the children have completed their work, talk with the class about the many different ways that were used to show the same pattern.

How do we know that these are the same basic pattern? Can you think of any place you have seen this pattern? [wrapping paper, wallpaper, tiled floors, fabric]

Throughout the year continue to give the children opportunities to translate patterns into different media, using both repeating patterns and growing patterns in concrete, pictorial, and symbolic forms. Be certain to discuss the various representations of the same pattern.

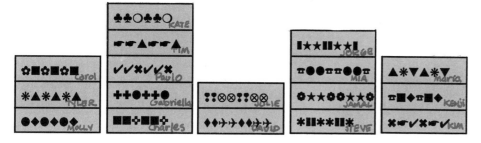

Help children make connections between their work with patterns and their strategies for solving varied mathematical problems.

"Sean's mother left him a note to pack an apple and two cookies in each of the three lunch bags. Draw a picture to show what the bags will contain."

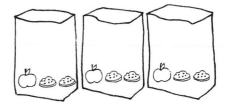

"Kara is collecting aluminum cans to recycle. For three weeks she brought 3 cans on each Monday and 2 cans on each Thursday. In three weeks, how many cans did she bring?"

$$3 + 2 = 5 \quad 3 + 2 = 5 \quad 3 + 2 = 5$$
$$5 + 5 + 5 = 15$$

● ★ ● ★ ● ★ ● *is an example of an AB pattern.*

♥ ⊗ ⊗ ♥ ⊗ ⊗ *is an example of an ABB pattern.*

✖ ✖ ✔ ✔ ✖ ✖ *is an example of an AABB pattern.*

✿ ◆ ✿ ✿ ◆ ✿ ✿ ◆ *is an example of a growing pattern— ABAABAAAB.*

Assessment should incorporate multiple sources of information as students apply their understandings about patterns.

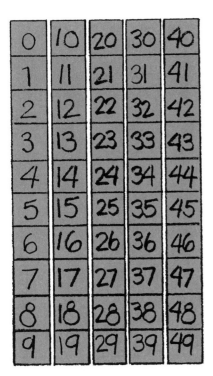

Post examples of different patterns and ask each child to choose one and translate it into a different representation. Make a large chart with sections labeled with each pattern.

Look at your pattern. Which basic pattern unit on the board is your pattern like? Show the class how you know where your pattern belongs.

After all children have identified the proper unit and group for their patterns, have them use their pattern units to make a display.

USING PATTERNS

Predictable Literature

Children enjoy listening to stories with a predictable pattern that repeats over and over, because they can "read" along with the teacher.

Get ready. The purpose of this activity is to have children recognize how patterns help them predict what will happen in a story. Predictable stories such as "The Little Red Hen," "The Gingerbread Man," and "The Three Billy Goats Gruff," are readily available. Some stories, such as "The House That Jack Built," have growing patterns.

Get going. After reading "The Little Red Hen," discuss the pattern in the questions asked by the hen and in the responses given by her friends. Have the children dramatize the story to show their understanding of the pattern.

Suppose the Little Red Hen had met a horse. What do you think the conversation would have been? Suppose she had met a cow?

Use other predictable books to furnish children with opportunities to focus on how patterns help them know what will happen.

Keep going. Have the children create their own predictable stories. As they begin, help them focus on a repeating unit or on a growing pattern.

As you make up your predictable story, what do you need to think about? What will be repeating in your story?

When the children have written and illustrated their own stories, have them make books. Put these into a class library, and share them with other classes.

PATTERNS WITH NUMBERS

Get ready. The purpose of this activity is to have children recognize and generate number sequences.

Each child will need either a long paper strip, such as adding-machine tape, that has been folded or marked in equal units or five strips of large grid paper ten units long; counters; construction paper for a background; and glue.

Get going. If using ruled-off adding-machine tape, have each student make a long tape that shows counting by ones from 0 to 49. Be certain that they write only one number in each section. Then, have the children cut their strips apart into five columns, cutting between 9 and 10, 19 and 20, 29 and 30, and 39 and 40.

◆　　　◆　　　◆　　　◆　　　◆　　　◆　　　◆　　　◆

If using the ten-unit grid strips, have the children write from 0 to 9 on the first strip, 10 to 19 on the second, and so on, through 40 to 49.

Lay your strips end to end on the floor in one long line. What kind of pattern do you see in the digits in the ones place?

Is there a pattern in the tens place?

What would the digits in the ones place be if I continued counting forward?

Have the children glue their strips side by side on construction paper, carefully lining up the rows next to each other.

What patterns do you see on the chart you have made? Do you see any patterns that go across the paper? That go down the paper?

Put a marker on every 2. Does this make a pattern?

What do you think you will see if we put markers on every 4? On every 7?

Suppose we wanted to count to 99 on our charts. How would the next column begin? Do you know where 65 will be? How do you know? Will 83 be in the top row if I keep on counting on the chart? Why or why not?

Keep going. Show the students how to count with their calculators. Tell them to push ⊞ ①　〓 on their calculators. The number 1 will appear on the display. Next have them push 〓 again. The display will show 2. Have them continue to punch 〓 .

What is happening as you push the equals key? Let's see if our calculators will count by fives. Push the clear button. Now push ⊞ ⑤ 〓. What do you see? What do you think will happen if you push the equals key again?

Have the students continue to explore counting by fives.

Clear your calculators. If you push ⊞ ⑤ 〓, remember that you will first see a 5. Try this. What do you think you will see if you push the equals key three more times? Tell me what number appears on the display if you start over and push the equals key a total of five times. What is the pattern when we count by fives?

How do you think we can make the calculator count by tens? Could we make it count by twos? How can we find out? If we count by twos, do you think that 34 is one of the numbers we will get? How do you know?

Is 78 one of the numbers we get when we count by tens? If your calculator shows 30 and you are counting by tens, how many more times will you punch the equals key to get to 100?

Counting by 1s, 2s, 5s, 10s, or any other number can be easily accomplished by using a calculator with a constant key function. Most four-function calculators have this feature. For example, punching ⊞ ② 〓 〓 〓 〓 〓 〓 generates the sequence 2, 4, 6, 8, 10, 12. Punching ⊞ ⑤ 〓 〓 〓 〓 〓 displays the sequence 5, 10, 15, 20, 25.

Different calculators may require other keystrokes to count by a given number. ③ ⊞ 〓 〓 gives 3, 6, 9. Let students explore alternative ways to use their calculators.

NUMBER SENSE AND OPERATIONS

Children who have number sense understand how numbers relate to each other and furnish information about the world. Number sense evolves from a child's total experiences as well as through specific activities. When first-grade children count things in the classroom or explore the operations of addition and subtraction, they are extending their earlier ideas of number. When they organize and compare groups of objects and examine multiple representations of the same numbers, they continue to broaden their understandings. These new ideas about number relationships provide a foundation for understanding number magnitude, estimation, and the effects of arithmetic operations. These early experiences in measurement pave the way for more formal investigations later on. When given an opportunity to explore and experiment, children demonstrate an increasing ability to use numbers in and outside school.

Children need to be encouraged to talk and write about what they have learned. When many of us were in school, doing mathematics was a silent pencil-and-paper occupation. Since that time, however, researchers have found that most children learn best if they discuss their work. Other studies also indicate that pencil-and-paper activities should follow extensive exploration of numerical relationships with manipulatives.

In the following set of activities, children use materials, such as beans and dominos, to investigate ideas about number. Because the children are learning through active involvement with manipulatives, they will be better able to demonstrate and communicate their knowledge.

You need to illustrate for parents how children are using these materials to learn mathematical concepts. You might send them a special newsletter, have a family mathematics night program, or create a special mathematics display for an open house. Children can make many samples for their parents to enjoy. For example, have children glue toothpicks on a file card and use numbers to describe the designs in various ways.

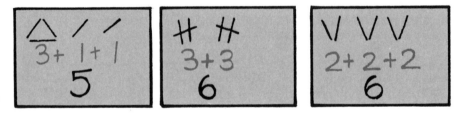

The activities with the computer using the Logo programming language furnish opportunities for linking concrete experiences with more abstract mathematics. Such bridges help students understand the concepts involved. They also help students appreciate the connections between what they study in school and the multiple uses of numbers in the world.

RELATING COUNTING AND OPERATIONS

Ladybugs and Leaves

Get ready. The purpose of this activity is to have children investigate the different ways a number can be expressed as the sum of two addends.

Children must understand numbers if they are to make sense of the ways numbers are used in their everyday world. (NCTM 1989a, p. 38)

A first-grade teacher relates, "Yesterday my lesson was on estimation and how to make a smart guess. The kids enjoyed guessing my age. I had guesses between 19 and 88! Then I gave them clues like 'my grandmother is 81 and my mom is 46.' You could see the wheels turning. Finally someone guessed 26! I am always nervous when someone asks me to estimate. I can't remember estimating when I was in school. I'm glad things have changed."

Discuss the nature and the value of these activities with parents. A rich understanding of number forms the basis for counting, arithmetic, and real-world applications. Children need experiences with manipulatives to develop number sense—paper-and-pencil work alone is not sufficient for most children.

Use the blackline master on page 11 to make a workmat for each child. Each child also needs ten beans, which can be painted to look like ladybugs. To make ladybugs, spray-paint lima beans red and dot them with a permanent marker to make the spots. You may also use red cubes or other counters for your ladybugs.

Get going. Distribute the workmats and the ladybugs. Plan time for the children to play with their materials. Suggest that they make up stories to act out for each other.

Bring the group together by telling the children a story that you have made up about six ladybugs. Ask them to model your story by putting three ladybugs on each leaf and putting the rest of their ladybugs away.

Can you put the ladybugs on the leaves in another way? How many different arrangements can you find? (Consider 1 + 5 and 5 + 1 as different arrangements.)

Record the children's findings on the chalkboard. If the children suggest arrangements in random order, talk with them about ways to organize the list.

Challenge them to find and record all possible arrangements. Have them work in pairs to decide if they have found all possible combinations. After they have written the combinations and organized the data, encourage them to find the patterns that emerge. For example, students may notice that as the first number (addend) gets smaller by 1, the second number (addend) gets larger by 1. Others may say that the answer (sum) is always 6.

Keep going. Ask the children if they can predict the number of possible arrangements for different numbers of ladybugs.

Do you think that larger numbers have more arrangements than smaller numbers? How could we find out? Let's try it with three ladybugs. How many ways can you arrange them? Now try four ladybugs.

Show students how to make a chart for recording their findings when they experiment with the ladybugs on the workmats.

How many arrangements are there for five? For six? For seven?

Can you predict how many there will be for eight? For twenty-two? How did you figure that out?

The ladybugs can also be used for a variety of other explorations, such as the following readiness activity for missing addend and comparison subtraction problems. Give the children ten ladybugs and a workmat. Ask them to place four ladybugs on one leaf. Then ask,

How many will be on the other leaf?

If you have eight ladybugs altogether and three of them are on one leaf, how many are on the other leaf?

Let the children explore missing addends and comparisons with other numbers and discuss their strategies for solving the problems. For example, you might say,

Organizing the number sentences in a structured format helps students find all the combinations and discover the resulting patterns.

$$6 + 0 = 6$$
$$5 + 1 = 6$$
$$4 + 2 = 6$$
$$3 + 3 = 6$$
$$2 + 4 = 6$$
$$1 + 5 = 6$$
$$0 + 6 = 6$$

Number of ladybugs	Ways to arrange ladybugs
3	4
4	5
5	?
6	?

One way to assess a child's understanding of the number relationships explored in these activities is to present a new material, such as interlocking cubes, and ask the child to demonstrate several ways a given number, such as 5, can be shown.

This activity makes connections between counting, developing patterns, and organizing data.

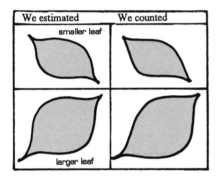

Times of free exploration offer many opportunities to informally evaluate individual students' understanding of mathematical ideas. While children are engaged with the materials, move around the classroom to assess students' use of various counting strategies or their understanding of "more," "less," and "the same."

If there are six ladybugs on one leaf and nine on the other, how many more ladybugs are there on the second leaf?

How Many Ladybugs?

Get ready. The purpose of this activity is to give children opportunities to estimate, count, and group objects. Complete this investigation with the class before children work independently on similar tasks.

Use the ladybugs and the leaf workmat from the previous lesson. Have the children work in pairs. Give a recording sheet to each pair of children.

Get going. Ask each pair of students to estimate the number of ladybugs needed to cover the smaller leaf. Have them talk about their answer and write down their mutual estimate. Tell the students to cover the smaller leaf with ladybugs.

When we cover our leaves, do you think all of us will use the same number of ladybugs for the smaller leaf? Why or why not?

How many ladybugs did you use? Is that more or fewer than you guessed? Would it take more or fewer ladybugs if you used very large ones to cover your leaves?

Have the children record their count and repeat the activity by estimating how many ladybugs it will take to cover the other leaf, recording their estimate, covering the second figure, counting the number of ladybugs, and recording the actual count.

Was your estimate for the second leaf closer than your first estimate? Why do you think this happened?

Keep going. Ask the students to group the ladybugs by fives.

If you count them by fives, do you think you will have the same total that you had when you counted by ones?

Have the children experiment with grouping the ladybugs and counting by twos and tens.

Because children learn through multiple experiences and enjoy similar activities using different materials, you may want to repeat these lessons with other manipulatives. Instead of ladybugs and leaves, you might try blocks in two boxes or paper fish in two ponds. Using animal-shaped cereal as counters appeals to children, especially when the children are allowed to eat the manipulatives at the end of the lesson. Directions may be written on task cards to make the activity appropriate for an independent center.

Domino Fun

Get ready. The purpose of this activity is to have children develop an understanding of number relationships and of ordering numbers. Have the students work in pairs, sharing a set of dominoes; each child will need a copy of the blackline master Domino Record Sheet (p. 11).

Get going. Hold up a domino and have the children tell the total number of dots. Then ask them to find a domino that has more dots and to find another that has fewer dots.

Hold up a domino and ask the children to find a domino that has one dot more and to find another that has one dot less.

Did all of you find the same domino? How are they different? How are they all the same?

Is there a domino for which you cannot find another domino with more dots? With fewer dots?

I am thinking of a domino that has five dots. What could it look like? Record the possibilities on the board.

How many dots would the domino have if it had one more dot? What would it look like? Is there more than one answer?

I have another domino. If you added one more dot, there would be eight dots altogether. What domino could I have? Draw the possibilities as students suggest the various dominoes that have seven dots.

Give the students a copy of the blackline master. Demonstrate how to draw a domino and record the solutions. Notice that the blackline master, with your modifications, can be used in a variety of ways, some very structured and others more open-ended.

Keep going. Select two dominoes that have the same number of dots and lay one on top of the other as shown.

If you know that both dominoes have the same number of dots, how many dots must be covered up?

How many different problems could we make with these two dominoes by covering up different parts?

STEPPING

Get ready. The purposes of this activity are to have children follow directions, estimate, measure and describe geometric paths, and carry out a computer algorithm.

Children will need a copy of the blackline master Turtle Time (p. 12) and access to a computer. A computer with a large screen or a display unit for use with an overhead projector is ideal for whole-class computer work, although first-graders willingly gather around a small screen.

Get going. Ask the class, *How many heel-to-toe steps do you think it would take to go across the classroom?* Record their estimates and have the children check their guesses by walking. Repeat with other distances and locations.

Everyone stand up and spread out. Guess where you would be if you walked forward eight steps. Try it.

Imagine you are at a street corner and want to make a right turn. Point in the direction you would be facing. Go ahead and turn right. Turn right again. Once more. How many right turns did it take to turn all the way around?

Give other similar directions; include left turns, turning halfway around, and so on.

Domino Record Sheet

My domino	Total dots	One less	One more	My domino	Total dots	One less	One more
⚁	3	2	4		—	—	—
	—	—	—		—	—	—
	—	—	—		—	—	—
	—	—	—		—	—	—
	—	—	—		—	—	—

"There are seven dots on my top domino. I can see four on the bottom, so there must be three hidden."

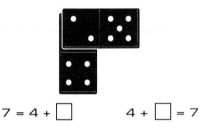

$$7 = 4 + \square \qquad 4 + \square = 7$$

Missing addend situations can be true problem-solving activities for first-graders.

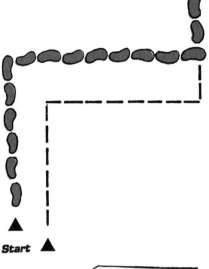

Start ▲

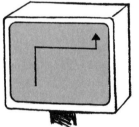

Face me. Guess where you would be if you walked forward five steps, turned right, and walked forward five steps again. Try it.

If you had been walking in the sand, what path would your footprints have left? Have the students describe and draw this path. Repeat with other directions.

Write the following directions on the chalkboard or an overhead transparency:

1. Mark a starting place.
2. Take 6 heel-and-toe steps forward.
3. Turn right.
4. Walk forward 8 heel-and-toe steps.
5. Turn left.
6. Walk forward 2 heel-and-toe steps.

Try to imagine someone following these directions and leaving a path. What will this path look like?

Discuss the students' ideas. Select a student to follow the directions. Draw a representation of this student's path on the board and review the directions that created it.

Show the children how to turn on the computer and load Logo. Demonstrate simple Logo commands and explain how they make the turtle move. Show the students the following sequence of commands:

FD 60
RT 90
FD 80
LT 90
FD 20

How does the turtle's path compare with the path we walked? How are they alike? How are they different? Why? Encourage the children to use numbers and directions in their answers.

If you change a command, will the path drawn be the same or different? Why?

Change the FD 20 to FD 50, and ask the students to predict the path. Clear the screen and type this new sequence of commands to check their predictions. Repeat, changing LT 90 to RT 90.

Keep going. Have pairs of students complete the blackline master Turtle Time.

Encourage further interaction with the computer world of Logo by asking such questions as these:

How could you make the turtle walk other paths? Can you make it draw a square? A triangle? A rectangle? How many steps did you use?

Can you make the turtle draw a letter? Your initials?

Domino Record Sheet

My domino	Total dots	One less	One more	My domino	Total dots	One less	One more
⬜⬜	_____	_____	_____	⬜⬜	_____	_____	_____
⬜⬜	_____	_____	_____	⬜⬜	_____	_____	_____
⬜⬜	_____	_____	_____	⬜⬜	_____	_____	_____
⬜⬜	_____	_____	_____	⬜⬜	_____	_____	_____
⬜⬜	_____	_____	_____	⬜⬜	_____	_____	_____

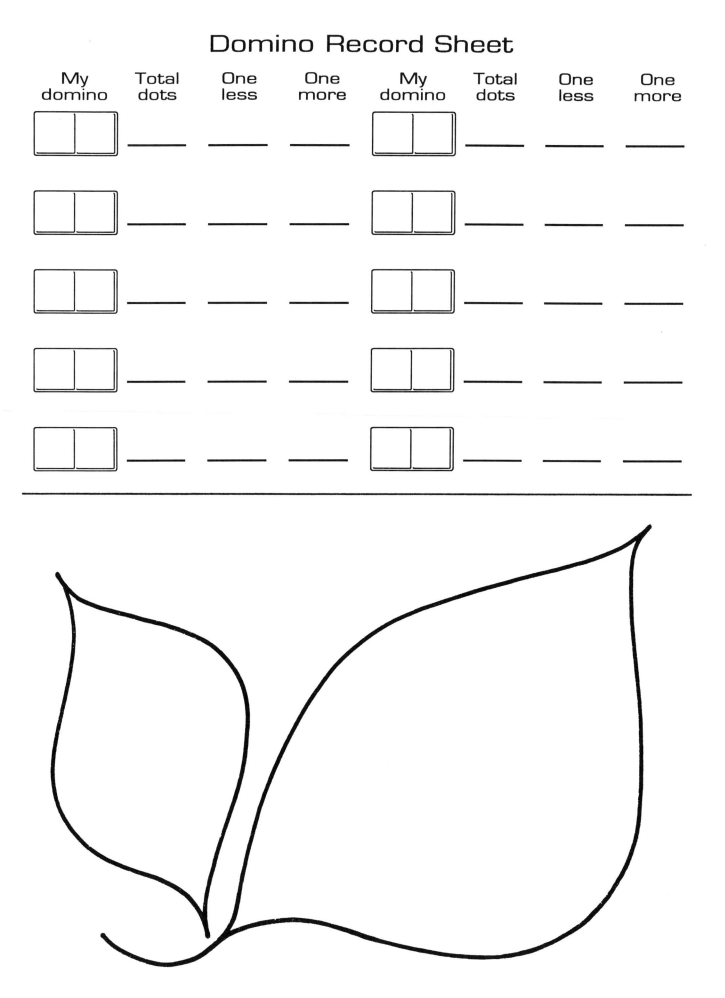

Turtle Time

In the Classroom: Child Steps

A. You are the turtle.

Walk the path.

1. FD 5
2. RT 90
3. FD 5
4. RT 90
5. FD 5
6. RT 90
7. FD 5

B. Draw your path.

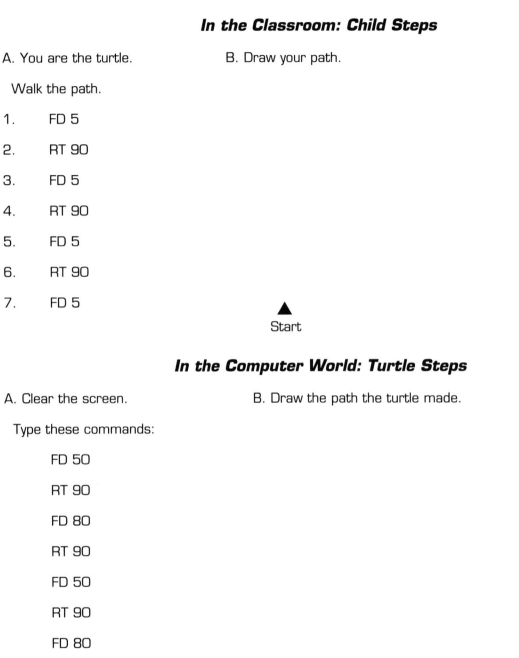

▲
Start

In the Computer World: Turtle Steps

A. Clear the screen.

Type these commands:

FD 50

RT 90

FD 80

RT 90

FD 50

RT 90

FD 80

RT 90

B. Draw the path the turtle made.

C. Clear the screen. Place a small piece of masking tape somewhere on the screen. Give the turtle commands that will make it hide under the masking tape on the screen. Could the turtle have gotten there with a shorter path?

◣ *MAKING SENSE OF DATA*

First grade is a wonderful time to help children make sense of data. Often more new information is presented at this grade level than at any other. As children learn to sort and organize, they develop extremely useful skills that will help them deal with the vast amount of information they will learn during their school years.

First-grade students are curious about themselves. The activities in "What We Think Counts!" capitalize on this interest by asking the children to make decisions about how they feel or choices about things they like. They are ready to explore new and different ways to organize, display, and interpret information.

In the activities described here, children move from making pictorial graphs to using graph paper. They also have experiences in extending their sorting skills to sets that overlap. That is, an object may belong in two categories at one time; for example, a child might belong in both categories "children who like apple pie" and "children who like cake."

To gather the information for one activity, the children measure lengths. In another, they tally to help count the number of things in the classroom.

The children are asked to discuss the graphs they have made. They are practicing not only their counting skills, but also their thinking skills as they compare graphs and predict what the graphs of other students who gathered the same information might look like.

WHAT WE THINK COUNTS!

Get ready. The purposes of this activity are to have children express opinions or feelings about different subjects and discuss their thoughts with each other. To help them see what other children are thinking, graph everyone's responses to the questions.

For the activities in this section, you will need 3" x 5" cards for each child, crayons, tacks or tape, and a space to display the cards, such as a bulletin board. Once the stage is set in the first activity, you can use many variations throughout the year. A suggestion is given for each month, which varies the topic, the number of choices, and the ways to handle the information. You will think of other ideas that will be more personalized than the ones given here.

Get going. Have each child draw a happy face on one side of a 3" x 5" card and a sad face on the other side and write his or her name on each side of the card.

Discuss with your class what makes people happy or sad. Give examples such as the following and let the children hold up either a happy face or a sad face to let you know how they feel:

> a sunny day
> a red flower
> someone hitting a dog
> trash on the floor
> children sharing toys

Children need to recognize that many kinds of data come in many forms and that collecting, organizing, displaying, and thinking about them can be done in many ways. (NCTM 1989a, p. 54)

Interacting with classmates helps children construct knowledge, learn other ways to think about ideas, and clarify their own thinking. (NCTM 1989a, p. 26)

Turn the discussion to things that can make some people happy and some people sad. If you have a story about rain, read it to the children.

Have the children decide whether they would be happy or sad if it were raining now. They should turn their cards to display how they are feeling. Place the cards on a bulletin board or a wall as shown above.

How many happy faces are there? Sad faces?

Does that tell us how many children in the class are feeling happy about the rain? Sad about the rain? Have the children who put up happy faces stand; count them to show that the numbers match.

How many more children are feeling happy than sad? Sad than happy? How can we tell?

Do you think if we do this tomorrow, the graph will look the same?

Keep going. Each month, make and discuss another graph for which the children must make a decision. Here are some ideas:

October: *Would you rather make a jack-o'-lantern with a happy face, a sad face, or a scary face?* Give the children jack-o'-lantern outlines and let them fill in the faces. After making a graph of the jack-o'-lanterns, discuss how many there are of each type and look for other differences —did anyone put on noses? Ask for suggestions about other ways to sort the jack-o'-lanterns.

November: *Would you rather have been a pilgrim or an Indian at the first Thanksgiving dinner?* Have the children draw a pilgrim's hat or a feathered headdress on happy faces.

December: *Which of these three desserts is your favorite?* Write the names of three desserts on the board; have the children put a happy face above their choice. After discussing this graph ask, *Which dessert do you like the least?* Write the names of the desserts on the board again and have the children put a sad face above their least favorite. Discuss how the two graphs are alike and are different. For example, in the graph below about the same number of children chose apple pie as their favorite dessert and as their least favorite dessert.

January: *What color scarf and what color hat would you put on your snowman or snow woman—red or green?* Give the children a drawing of a snow figure and a red and a green crayon. After they have colored the scarf and the hat, let the children discuss how to sort and graph the figures. There are four categories: red hat and red scarf, red hat and green scarf, green hat and red scarf, and green hat and green scarf.

February: *What is your favorite number from 0 through 9?* First, have the children describe what they think the graph will look like—"lots of blocks colored for fives," "no zeros," "about the same for each number." Then, have the children color in a block (or draw a happy face) above their favorite number on the prepared graph.

Ask the children if they think their class is like other classes. Work with another teacher to do the same activity with his or her class. Post both results outside the classrooms, and have the children compare the two graphs.

March: *If it were possible, would you rather fly on an airplane, a hot air balloon, a magic rug, or a rocket?* Make a happy face graph. As the children discuss the graph, have them tell why they made their choice, what they think they would see, and where they would go.

April: *Do you like to play tag or hide-and-seek?* (Choose two games that the children actually like.) Let the children say one or the other or both. Put out two large yarn circles, one for each game. Let the circles overlap slightly. Have the children stand inside the circle of the game that they like. If they like both, they should be inside both circles (i.e., the intersection). Discuss how many children liked *only* tag, liked *only* hide-and-seek, or liked both. Tell the children that it is difficult to count them when they all are standing, so you are going to help them make a picture. Make a chart and place sticky notes with the children's names in the appropriate places.

How many children are in the class? How many children liked tag? (Include all those in the "tag" circle.) *How many liked hide-and-seek?* Record these numbers. *Does 18 plus 22 equal the number in the whole class? Why or why not?*

May: *Which ice-cream flavors do you like—vanilla, chocolate, or strawberry?* Put out a big circle of white (vanilla) yarn, of brown (chocolate) yarn, and of pink (strawberry) yarn as shown in the picture. Have the children place their happy faces inside the circle of the ice cream flavor that they like. If they like chocolate and strawberry, they should be in the intersection of the brown and pink circles. If they like all three, they should be in the intersection of the white, brown, and pink circles.

Our Favorite Numbers

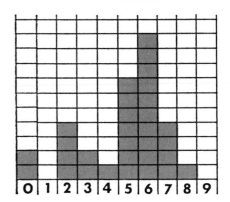

Children in the class: 26

Tag	Hide-and-Seek
18	22

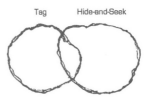

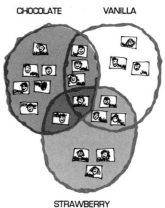

MY VERY OWN GRAPH

Get ready. The purpose of this activity is to have children measure and graph lengths and discuss their findings. The children should have had experience measuring lengths with connecting cubes and coloring in a bar graph to represent the data.

For this activity each child will need a sheet of Me, Myself, and I graph paper (blackline master on p.18), connecting cubes, and crayons.

Get going. Begin the activity by asking these questions:

How long are our feet, our big toes, our hands, and our thumbs? Do you think we have the same size feet? Let's figure out a way to show all our parents when they come to the PTA meeting next Tuesday. How could we leave a record for them to see?

After discussing the problem, bring the group to the idea of making a graph of the length of each child's foot, toe, hand, and thumb. Demonstrate with the cubes by making a tower as long as your hand.

Distribute Me, Myself, and I graph paper to the children. Illustrate how to color one space on the graph for each cube in the tower. Have the children complete the graphs.

Did everyone have the same foot length?

How many different sizes of big toes did we have?

What do you think the graph of our parents' feet, toes, hands, and thumbs would look like?

Find a partner. Figure out how your graphs are different and how they are the same.

Can you find someone who has a graph that looks exactly like yours?

Keep going. You may wish to have parents make a similar graph either at a PTA meeting or at home. Some parents' feet will be longer than the ten spaces on the graph. Let them record above the graph how many more spaces they need. Discuss with the children the differences and similarities between the parents' graphs and theirs.

THE BIG COUNT

Get ready. The purpose of this activity is to have children learn to make an inventory. They tally the number of objects in the classroom and then find the number in each category by counting. The calculator can be used for counting large numbers.

Use this activity near the end of the year when the counting skills of the students are more developed. The activity has several phases (deciding what to count, collecting data, and displaying results), which might be conducted over several days.

Get going. Discuss why stores take an inventory. Many children will have seen inventories being taken in grocery stores.

Tell the children that you want to find out how many things are in the classroom and you need their help. Let them decide what they want to count—desks, books, toys, coat hooks, tables, chairs, games. Make a list of what they suggest, adding ideas if they need prompting. If there are places that are off-limits (files in cabinets, your desk), make that clear from the beginning.

If the children have not used tallying, take some time to introduce the concept. For example, have a student clap while you demonstrate how to tally each clap on the chalkboard. When children first begin to tally, they may not see the basic pattern of four strokes down and one across. Be aware that some may become engrossed in downward strokes and forget to make the group of five; others may make five downward strokes and cross them with a sixth mark. Tell them that when people take an inventory, they often keep a tally because if they count without a written record, they often lose their place.

Have two children demonstrate keeping a tally. One points to the object and the other makes a tally mark. Let each child practice with a partner.

Before beginning the big count, divide the students into pairs and decide the category for each pair to count. For example, one pair may be responsible for the books on the third shelf and another pair may be responsible for the toy cars.

Assist with the tallying when necessary, but do not expect perfection at this age! The process of this activity is more important than a precise product. Movement and conversation are integral to the process.

Have the pair count their tallies. You may wish to help them count by fives or allow them to use the calculator. Use the constant key or press ⊞ 5 ⊟ ⊟. Every time the ⊟ key is hit, another 5 will be added. One child can point to a group of five, and the other can push the equals key.

Post the big counts. Discuss how many of each thing is in the room. Focus on such categories as—

> large and small numbers,
>
> numbers more than 100,
>
> the relationship between number and size (e.g., observe that twelve crayons occupy less space than twelve books).

Although the numbers may be quite large for some children, they may be able to make comparisons by looking at the tallies. For example, children might observe, " We don't have many games, but we have lots of books."

Keep going. Children may want to take an inventory of their rooms at home, their own books, or the types of vehicles they see pass a corner in an hour. Let them decide what they want to count.

Me, Myself, and I   **Name** _____

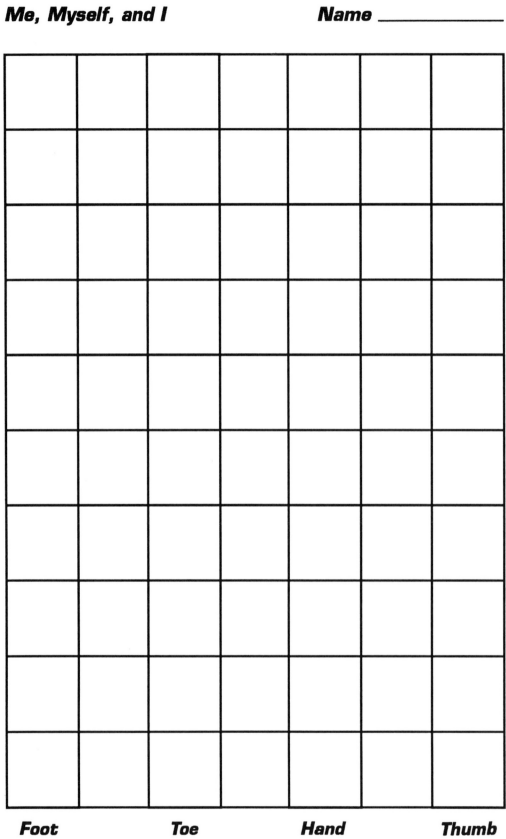

Foot   **Toe**   **Hand**   **Thumb**

GEOMETRY AND SPATIAL SENSE

We live in a world of patterns, shapes, and movement—that is, a world of geometry. Because young children are naturally fascinated with their surroundings and are constantly receiving information through sight, touch, sound, and movement, their spatial capabilities usually exceed their numerical skills. Spatial sense involves perceptual abilities that are important for early school success. Such success has a strong influence on the child's self-concept and stability.

A large portion of a child's early behavior is essentially spatial in character. This behavior is prelinguistic because a child first encounters and explores the world without the benefit of language. Although children in grade 1 are learning to read and write, these skills are frequently not developed enough to allow the children to follow more than the simplest written instructions. For this reason, some lessons in this book depend on the teacher's oral instructions. We recognize the importance of language development and include a language component in many activities. In these, children are encouraged to express themselves in their own words before they are given the correct mathematical language. The activities may also encourage children to justify their choices or answers as they discuss them with you and their peers.

This informality should be the keystone of early geometry experiences. Children have observed geometry in their world since birth and have already acquired some strong ideas that need to be explored for validity. Hence a variety of experiences investigating and discussing geometric concepts in different contexts is needed.

SORTING PLANE AND SOLID FIGURES

Get ready. The purpose of this activity is to have children recognize that objects in a class are alike in some way(s) and can be distinguished from other objects. This spatial ability is called visual discrimination.

Get going. Have the children make a collection of objects from home or the classroom and cut pictures from magazines. Ask the children to describe where they found the objects and how they were used. Have them sort the objects and pictures according to shape.

Are there any other ways you could sort them? What will you do if some of the figures belong in more than one group?

Use the collections in a variety of ways:

Make a display with the objects. Label the different groups.

Make buildings or animals using different three-dimensional figures.

Have the children make class books shaped like a triangle, a rectangle, a square, and a circle. Fill each book with pictures of objects that have the shape of the book.

Turn a figure into the central feature of a picture. For example, paste a triangle on a sheet of paper and add details to show a picture of a tower, a clown face, or a house. Repeat for other figures.

As a class, make models shaped like a cube, a cylinder, a box, and a sphere.

Children should be encouraged to justify their solutions.... Manipulatives and other physical models help children relate processes to their conceptual underpinnings and give them concrete objects to talk about in explaining and justifying their thinking. (NCTM, 1989a, p. 29)

Identifying two-dimensional and three-dimensional figures in the environment gives children an opportunity to see which ones are most common and to see the many ways some (e.g., rectangles) are used.

Children's geometric ideas can be developed by having them sort and classify models of plane and solid figures,... , making drawings,.... (NCTM 1981a, p. 49)

Triangles and rectangles can vary in shape. For example:

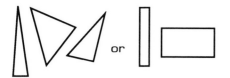

This is not possible with squares or circles. Children should recognize and discuss this concept.

Keep going. Have the children make pictures with figures. Ask them to cut out many different sizes and shapes of one figure, for example, triangles. These figures may be cut from paper, cloth, and so on. Let the children make a picture by sticking these figures to a large sheet of paper. Ask them to tell a story about their pictures.

What figures have you used? Do they all look exactly alike?

Have the children cut out several triangles, squares, circles, and rectangles and use them to make linear patterns. An example is shown below.

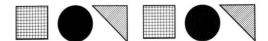

Notice that this pattern uses congruent figures, so the pattern is visually obvious. The next pattern (triangle, circle, rectangle) requires the child to retain the attributes of the figures in memory while testing each successive element to see if it adheres to the pattern. That is, the child must recognize that any triangle followed by any circle followed by any rectangle continues the pattern.

PROBLEM SOLVING WITH GEOBOARDS

Get ready. The purposes of this activity are to have children distinguish similarities and differences among geometric figures (visual discrimination) and to promote eye-hand coordination.

Give the children 5 x 5 geoboards and rubber bands. If you do not have enough geoboards, children can work in pairs.

A geoboard is an excellent manipulative to use in the early grades. It enables students to be better risktakers because errors are easy to correct and no evidence of incorrect drawings remains. Students at this level usually do not have the fine muscle skills required to write or draw well. Problems posed on the geoboard can be very simple, but with slight modification can be made more challenging.

The problems in this activity are designed for use with a 5 x 5 geoboard (25 pegs). If a board with fewer pegs is used, some of the problems will be impossible. If a board with more pegs is used, some of the problems will be too easy to be challenging. You should adjust the problems accordingly.

Rubber band touches:
3 pegs   4 pegs   5 pegs

Get going. Use the following activities to teach the meaning of the "boundary" of a plane figure. Note that the boundary will be used in later grades to determine perimeter. Look for different answers to each problem. Children should begin to realize that not all problems have just one correct answer and some problems may have no answer.

Have the children make a triangle on a 5 x 5 geoboard.

How many pegs does the rubber band touch? Make three triangles so that the rubber band touches three pegs, four pegs, and five pegs. Can you make a triangle so that the rubber band touches more pegs?

Is it possible to make a triangle that touches only two pegs? Is it possible to make a triangle that has the same number of pegs on two sides? On three sides?

Have the children share their solutions with each other. Discuss why three is the fewest number of pegs the rubber band can touch when a triangle is made.

Make a square with the rubber band touching four pegs and a square with the rubber band touching eight pegs. What other squares can you make? Count the number of pegs on each side. Discuss why each side must have the same number of pegs. Establish a pattern with the number of pegs on the boundary of a square: 4, 8, 12....

Explore rectangles the same way. Help the children to see that the number of pegs may not be the same for all four sides but will be the same for opposite sides.

Once the children have grasped the idea of pegs on the boundary, illustrate what is meant by "pegs inside." Point out that although the pegs touching the rubber band are technically "inside," for this problem we will count only those pegs that are not touching the rubber band.

Ask the children to make a triangle with two pegs inside, then with three pegs inside. *What is the greatest number of pegs that can be inside a triangle on a geoboard?*

Answers

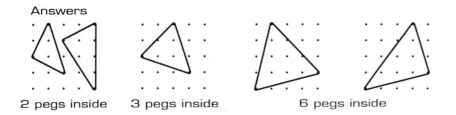

2 pegs inside   3 pegs inside   6 pegs inside

Repeat these problems using other figures, such as four-sided figures, and six-sided figures. *Is it possible to get more pegs inside a four-sided or a five-sided figure?* Note that the answers will vary according to the figures the children make.

Keep Going. Vary the characteristics of the figures as you present more problems—the number of sides, the number of pegs inside, and the number of pegs on the boundary. For example,

Make a triangle with one peg inside
and four pegs touching the rubber band."

As you repeat the directions for these problems, the children will see that there are three things to remember: the number of sides, the number of pegs inside the figures, and the number of pegs in the boundary. Initially it may be helpful to display the numbers in a chart.

Number of sides	Number of pegs inside	Number of pegs on the boundary
3	1	4
3	2	3
4	0	4

Let the children suggest other problems. Some problems may be impossible—for example, a triangle touching five pegs with two pegs inside. Exploring such possibilities gives children experience with problems that have no solution.

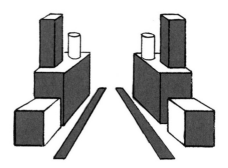

BUILDING TOWERS

Get ready. The purpose of this activity is to give children experiences in recognizing reflections and rotations.

Place two strips of masking tape about twenty centimeters apart on a table top to represent a road. Give the children cubes and assorted solids to construct "buildings" such as those illustrated.

Get going. Say to the children, *As you walk down this road you see a building on the left and one on the right. They look the same.* Show the children two identical buildings that are reflections of each other. Ask the children what they notice about the buildings. *How are they alike? How do they look different?* Point out that when you use the same blocks to build buildings that face the opposite way, you create mirror images. Use a mirror to demonstrate the reflections for the children.

To develop spatial sense, children must have many experiences that focus on geometric relationships; the direction, orientation and perspective of objects in space .... (NCTM 1989a, p. 49)

Gradually add to the buildings, placing a block on one side of the "road" and its matching block on the other side to make mirror images. After you have placed a few blocks, have the children take turns placing blocks.

If possible, take the children for a walk through the neighborhood and notice houses or buildings that are built side by side. Sometimes two buildings may look the same. A duplex or two houses that share a common driveway may illustrate mirror images. You may wish to collect data about the structures in the neighborhood and make a graph of the types of homes, stores, and other buildings.

Divide the class into pairs. Each pair should have the same set of three-dimensional blocks or other building materials. One child builds a tower with blocks on one side of the street. The other child builds a tower that is the mirror image on the other side of the street.

These experiences allow children to develop more complete understandings about shapes and their properties and to build the vocabulary of geometry in a natural manner. (NCTM 1989a, p. 49)

How could you use the mirror to check your buildings? Describe the building you have made. What kind of building did you make?

Repeat the activity with the students reversing roles.

Use this activity to explore other language relevant to position in space, such as right, left, in front of, behind, above, and below.

Keep going. This activity gives students the opportunity to devise their own language in a game situation. The children will recognize some of the problems in communicating descriptions of their towers and may ask for more precise terms.

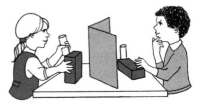

Place two children with a screen between them. Give each child the same two, three, four, or five solids. Child A builds a tower that child B cannot see. Child A describes the tower to child B, who attempts to build an identical one. The screen is removed and the towers are compared. A variation of the activity that may help in the beginning is to allow the second child to ask questions that may be answered by "yes" or "no" while he or she is trying the build the design.

Repeat the activity and have the children interchange roles. The children can later play this game on their own. Observing children during this activity and noting the ways they describe various figures and their orientations can be helpful in assessing their vocabulary.

DRAWING FROM MEMORY

Get ready. The purpose of this activity is to develop children's ability to copy figures from memory.

Prepare a transparency of simple designs such as those illustrated.

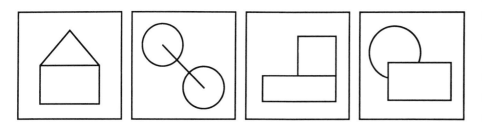

Use the blackline master on page 24 to make a copy of John's house for the overhead projector. Reproduce sufficient copies of the small drawings on the blackline master so that when the pictures are cut apart there is a copy of each picture for each child.

Get going. Use the projector to show the children one of the simple designs for a few seconds. Have them draw the design from memory. *How did you decide what to draw?* Show the transparency again and encourage the children to compare their drawings with the design. Repeat the activity with the other designs.

Give each child a copy of Joe's drawing. Tell them that Joe was copying the drawing of John's house and did not have time to finish. Show John's house on the overhead projector for two or three seconds. Cover the transparency and ask the students to complete Joe's drawing. When the students have done what they can, uncover the transparency and let the children compare their drawings with the original.

Repeat the activity using the incomplete drawings of Sam, Indira, and Josie. If the students find this to be an easy task, the four activities can be assigned in one lesson. For some students, the activities will need to be extended over several days. Since more details are omitted in progressing from Joe's drawing to Josie's, the children must remember more.

Keep going. For more activities of the same kind, use line drawings from a child's coloring book. Put the complete pictures on overhead transparencies. Put examples on a worksheet, eliminating different portions of the pictures each time.

This activity can be repeated periodically throughout the year. Increase the difficulty level as the children's abilities develop. Always encourage the children to talk about how they give themselves clues for remembering the designs.

Visual memory is the ability to recall accurately objects no longer in view. A person with exceptional visual memory may be endowed with a "photographic memory." Most students retain small amounts of visual information—about three to five items for short periods of time. This activity should help teachers assess their students' visual memory ability and suggest if further activities of this kind are needed to improve that ability.

Drawing and sketching shapes is an important part of developing spatial sense.... A figure is displayed on an overhead projector for two or three seconds and then the children try to draw the figure." (NCTM 1989a, p. 49)

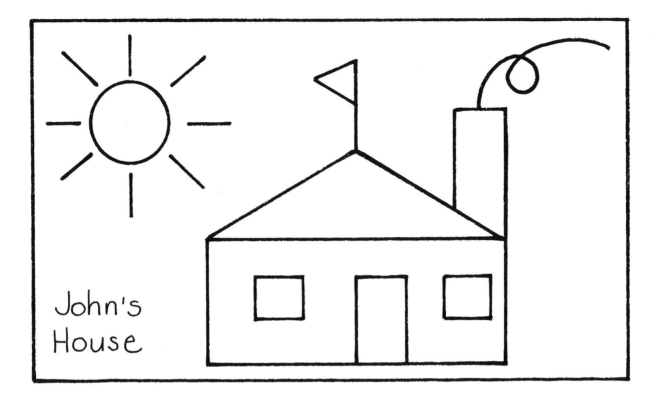

John's House

JOE

SAM

INDIRA

Josie